Whatever Happened to the Great Moderation?

Remarks at the 23rd Annual Hyman P. Minsky Conference
April 10, 2014

Jason Furman, Chairman, Council of Economic Advisers
As prepared for delivery

It is appropriate to use the occasion of the 23rd Annual Hyman Minsky Conference to discuss the topic of economic fluctuations, how they have evolved over time, and what we can and should do about them.

In the late 1990s, economists began a debate over what was termed the "Great Moderation," which refers to the reduction in the volatility of a wide range of economic variables, and to the associated increase in the longevity of economic expansions and reduction in the frequency and severity of economic contractions.[1] The debate was not over whether or not there was a Great Moderation—on the heels of the longest economic expansion in American history it was generally agreed that the fact was real, and the relatively mild recession in 2001 only further strengthened the belief. Instead the debate was over what caused it. Was it better monetary or fiscal policy? Or improved inventory management? Or expansions in consumer credit? Or just good luck?

The debate over the causes of the Great Moderation ended abruptly with the onset of the Great Recession in late 2007. With the worst economic crisis of our lifetimes still fresh in our minds, it shows little prospect of restarting anytime soon.[2] If anything, the media appears to have become increasingly sensitive to day-to-day fluctuations in the stream of economic data reports. It is easy to remember a lot of the recent volatility, whether it is the S&P 500 rising more than 1 percent after the initial estimate of fourth-quarter GDP growth came in above expectations this past January, or falling 2 percent just a week later, attributed to news of a large drop in the new orders subcomponent of the ISM manufacturing index.

In the wake of the Great Recession, it is worth reassessing the Great Moderation hypothesis and understanding what it means for policy going forward. Was the Great Moderation hypothesis spectacularly wrong, and did researchers miss the fact that the economy was increasingly unstable? After all, in addition to the Great Recession in the United States, we have also seen a number of serious banking and exchange rate crises in countries around the world over the last few decades. On the other hand, a number of key data series have exhibited a high degree of consistency and stability since the recovery began in mid-2009, and we are now two months away from what would be the longest streak of private-sector job growth on record. Is there a sense in which the Great Moderation has continued or returned? Even if we still see low volatility in the summary statistics we use to assess the Great Moderation, does this tell us

---

[1] Two of the earliest contributions were Kim and Nelson (1999) and McConnell and Perez-Quiros (2000). Blanchard and Simon (2001) and Stock and Watson (2003) were two of the more comprehensive and influential analyses. Some of the many other contributions include Kahn, McConnell and Perez-Quiros (2002), Bernanke (2004), Ahmed, Levin and Wilson (2004), and Dynan, Elmendorf and Sichel (2006).

[2] One notable exception is a recent working paper by Gadea, Gomez-Loscos and Perez-Quiros (2013).

something meaningful about the economy, or does it tell us more about the shortcomings of these summary statistics themselves?

In my remarks today, I will first explore what the original results on the Great Moderation look like with an additional ten to fifteen years of data, including the Great Recession.[3] I will also use these data to explore whether the factors that led economists to identify a Great Moderation are still present in the economy today, and whether the additional data affect our view of these factors. Second, I will sketch out some major problems with the Great Moderation hypothesis that have been highlighted by the Great Recession. Third, I will talk about why economic stability matters. I will end with a brief outline of the unfinished agenda to promote macroeconomic stabilization, focusing on areas outside of monetary policy that play an important but sometimes underappreciated role in fostering macroeconomic stability.

The President's economic agenda is focused on returning the economy more quickly to its full potential, expanding that potential growth over time, and ensuring that everyone shares in that economic growth. Putting in place steps that would reduce the likelihood of recessions, reduce their severity when they do occur, and better protect people from their consequences, would help advance all of these goals. Looking at how volatility has changed over time will help improve our understanding of the steps we need to take.

The Great Moderation in Normal Times

To start, I am going to take the previous definitions of the Great Moderation as given and ask whether or not it has continued based on those definitions. As I discuss in the next section, I believe that this exercise may tell us as much about the limitation of these measures as it does about actual structural trends in the economy. With that said, Figure 1a shows the volatility of output growth in the United States, measured by a twenty-quarter rolling standard deviation of quarterly real GDP growth.[4] This figure was used by Olivier Blanchard, now the Chief Economist of the International Monetary Fund (IMF), and John Simon to motivate their 2001 study in the *Brookings Papers on Economic Activity*. This particular measure of volatility increased sharply in the Great Recession, but still remained below where it had been for most of the 1950s through the mid-1980s. Moreover, this measure of volatility has now fallen back to the levels during the canonical "Great Moderation" period from the mid-1980s through 2007. This pattern is similar to that of other advanced economies in recent decades, as shown in Figure 1b.

---

[3] I want to thank Matt Aks, Philip Lambrakos and Chase Ross at the Council of Economic Advisers for their contributions to this analysis.
[4] The picture is very similar even if one uses the geometric average of the income (GDI) and expenditure (GDP) sides of total output.

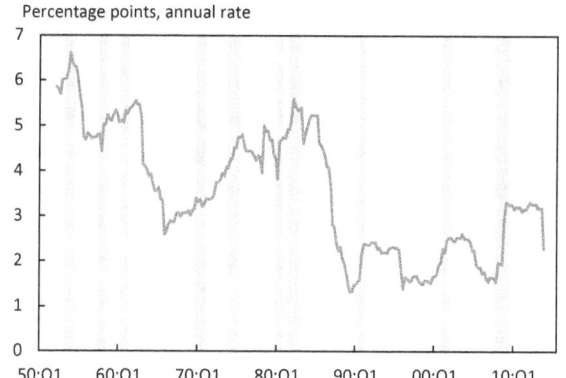

Figure 1a. Five-Year Rolling Standard Deviation of Quarterly Real GDP Growth

Percentage points, annual rate

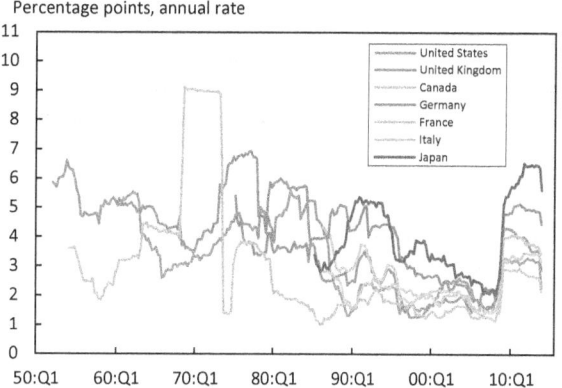

Figure 1b. Five-Year Rolling Standard Deviation of Quarterly Real GDP Growth, Comparison of G-7 Countries

Percentage points, annual rate

Another look at output volatility is provided by Table 1, which shows the mean and standard deviation of four-quarter GDP growth rates by decade. A version of this table initially appeared in a 2003 NBER *Macroeconomics Annual* paper written by Jim Stock, currently my colleague on the Council of Economic Advisers, and Mark Watson. This table shows a similar pattern, with a slight increase in volatility in the 2000-2013 period reflecting the Great Recession, but overall volatility still appears to be at a lower level than in the past.

Table 1. Mean and Standard Deviation of Four-Quarter Real GDP Growth

Period	Arithmetic Mean (Percent)	Standard Deviation (Percentage Points)
Full Sample (1960-2013)	3.1	2.3
1960s	4.5	2.0
1970s	3.2	2.7
1980s	3.1	2.7
1990s	3.2	1.5
2000-2013	1.9	1.9

Finally, comparing periods of economic expansions, we see that the general trend has been towards more consistent and less volatile recoveries. As shown in Figure 2, the standard deviation of quarterly GDP or monthly job growth is generally consistent with the pattern in the last two economic expansions, and well below the levels of volatility in earlier expansion periods. This fact is worth remembering the next time we are struck by a jobs report that comes in 50,000 above or below recent trends—this type of month-to-month noise is standard and if anything diminished from the typical fluctuations we experienced in the past.

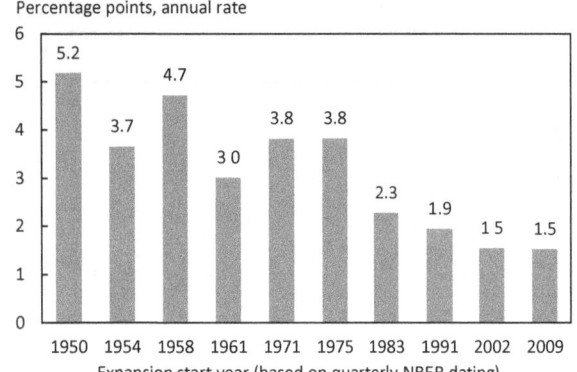

Figure 2a. Standard Deviation of Quarterly Real GDP Growth During Expansion Periods

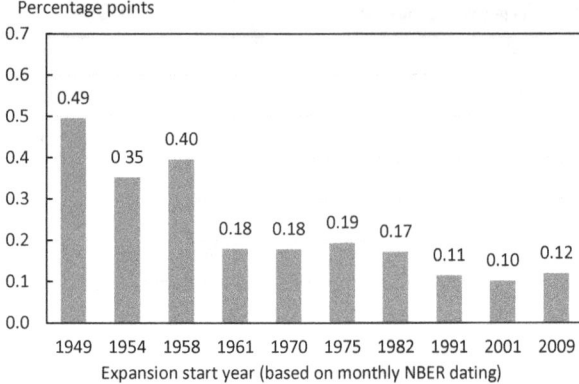

Figure 2b. Standard Deviation of Monthly Nonfarm Employment Growth During Expansion Periods

These various figures suggest that the features of the time series data that economists described as the Great Moderation have continued. But it still leaves open the question of whether the forces that produced less volatility pre-2007 have always been present, went away but have returned, or if new forces are at work. Just what were those forces that helped produce what was originally called the Great Moderation, and has another decade of data shed any more light on the debate? I will describe a few tentative conclusions here, recognizing that I am relying on relatively simple econometrics, considering data for only a relatively short period in some cases, and using a period that includes a very significant outlier event.

Is the Great Moderation Due to Reduced Shocks or Reduced Propagation of These Shocks?

The explanations originally offered for the Great Moderation were often summarized as good luck (i.e., fewer shocks), good policy (i.e., better ability to offset the shocks), or good structural changes (i.e., changes to features of the economy, like improved inventory management or composition shifts to less-volatile industries).

I would like to return to a key stylized fact that emerged in the literature, which is that the reduced variance of key macroeconomic data was associated with reductions in the volatility of the estimation errors in a time series model. To the extent these estimation errors are interpreted as "shocks," declining output volatility would reflect less volatile or less frequent "shocks," rather than a change in how the estimation errors, or shocks, are propagated through the economy over time. Another decade of data generally confirms and strengthens this original stylized fact. To illustrate this point, I update the simplest formulation of the stylized fact from Blanchard and Simon, estimating an equation that relates deviations in output growth from its trend to the first lagged deviation of output growth and a white noise shock term.[5] Specifically, I estimate an equation of the form:

$$(\Delta y_t - g) = a(\Delta y_{t-1} - g) + e_t$$

---

[5] Stock and Watson (2003) present results using more sophisticated statistical methods and a wider range of variables that largely confirm the original Blanchard and Simon (2001) analysis.

where y represents log output, g is the trend growth rate, a is a parameter that captures the persistence of output growth, and e is a white noise error term with variance σ.

In this formulation, a can be said to capture the underlying structure of the economy, while σ captures the nature of the shocks. If $a = 0$, then the volatility of output growth will exactly mirror the volatility of the underlying shocks. As a rises towards one, the total volatility of growth increasingly reflects some feature of the economy that makes shocks more persistent from one period to the next. Higher values of a indicate greater volatility, because growth depends not just on the shock in the given year, but also a compounding process that incorporates a weighted average of all the previous shocks as well.

The econometric estimates for rolling twenty-quarter estimates of the parameters a and σ are shown in Figures 3a and 3b. If anything, shocks appear to have become more persistent over the last decade—which by itself would actually increase overall volatility. Rather, consistent with the earlier results, the moderation in output volatility is driven by the reduction in the variance of the shocks themselves, which has greatly diminished over time and now stand around the same level as its postwar lows.

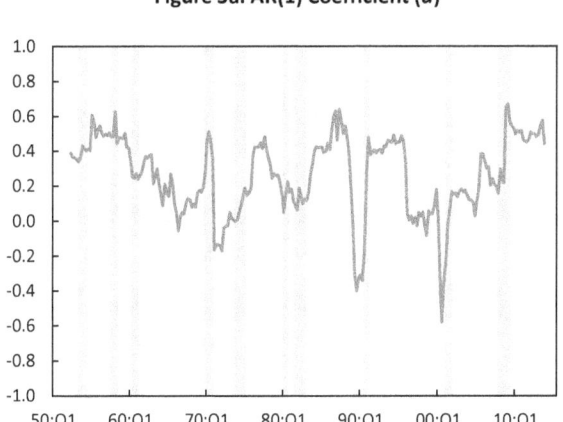

Figure 3a. AR(1) Coefficient (*a*)

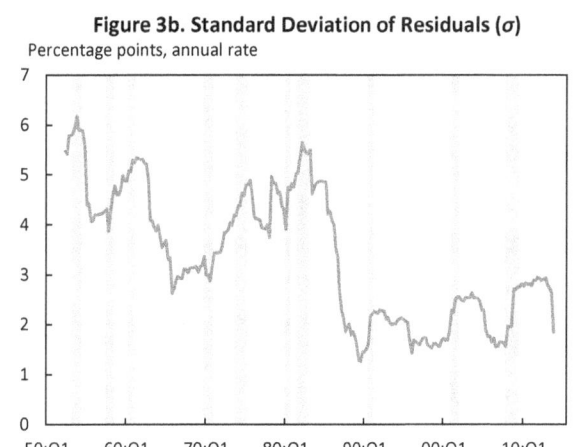

Figure 3b. Standard Deviation of Residuals (*σ*)

Percentage points, annual rate

What Is the Source of the Reduced Shocks?

By itself, this univariate approach says nothing about the source of the reduction in the volatility of shocks, since the error terms are by definition unexplained by the model. Stock and Watson (2003) generalize this approach to a multivariate vector autoregression using data through 2001, allowing their model to parse out specific shocks. They conclude that "the moderation in volatility is attributable to a combination of improved policy (10-25%), identifiable good luck in the form of productivity and commodity price shocks (20-30%), and other, unknown forms of good luck that manifest themselves as smaller reduced-form forecast errors (40-60%)."

One should be careful in interpreting these sorts of results—and Stock and Watson themselves offer a number of caveats to their analysis. The so-called "shocks" in this model are not necessarily truly independent from the structure of the economy itself; instead, they are errors in the structure that was assumed in the model. Some of these errors may represent genuine good or bad luck in the economic draw. But they likely represent much more than that.

As Ben Bernanke (2004) pointed out, more predictable monetary policy could lead to smaller measured "shocks" for a range of reasons, including fewer monetary disturbances and more anchored inflation expectations, as well as changes in wage and price setting institutions. To help illustrate this point, Bernanke cited work showing that seemingly exogenous "shocks" to oil prices in the 1970s could be in part traced to earlier monetary policy decisions. He also cited a series of papers showing that stable inflation expectations reduce the impact of exchange rate fluctuations. To the extent this factor contributes to smaller and less volatile shocks in an econometric model, we certainly would not want to attribute it solely to "good luck."

Finally, in spite of the econometric evidence, I do have some concern at an intuitive level about the view that the current expansion has been less volatile because of smaller and less frequent shocks. In actuality, we have seen a long list of shocks. This list includes international events like the European sovereign debt crisis, the tsunami and nuclear accident in Japan, and the disruption of Libya's oil supply. It includes extreme weather like Hurricane Sandy and the 2012 drought that was described by the USDA as the "most severe and extensive drought in at least 25 years."[6] And of course, it includes an unnecessary and unprecedented degree of brinksmanship in Congress' handling of federal fiscal policy, culminating in the 16-day shutdown last October.

One view is that, when examined systematically these shocks are not as large as we may have intuitively thought—that may be possible. But it is also certainly possible that our econometric models are failing to capture more subtle ways in which the structure of the economy has become more stable over time, the policy response to the crisis helped to pre-emptively mitigate subsequent shocks, or that a series of roughly equal-sized negative shocks will show up in the trend growth term rather than in the residual.

Does the Improved Inventory Management Hypothesis Hold Up?

Another decade of data calls into question one of the original explanations of the Great Moderation: improved inventory management.[7] These data should be taken cautiously because they cover only a short period of time, nevertheless they are suggestive. Table 2, which is based on analysis originally in Kahn, McConnell and Perez-Quiros (2002), decomposes the variance of goods output into three pieces: the variance of sales, the variance of the change in inventories, and the covariance of sales and inventories. From 1960 to 1984, inventories were quite volatile, and were also procyclical, meaning that when sales increased, inventories also increased, further contributing to the volatility of production.

During the post-1984 Great Moderation period, inventory investment itself became much less volatile, and the previous relationship between inventories and sales reversed, so that the two became negatively correlated. Focusing specifically on durable goods, the change in the covariance between inventories and sales accounts for nearly half of the decline in the variance

---

[6] See http://www.ers.usda.gov/topics/in-the-news/us-drought-2012-farm-and-food-impacts.aspx#.U0ay4PldXFk.

[7] In addition to the work cited in the text, see also Kahn and Stevens (2008), McCarthy and Zakrajsek (2007), and Morley and Singh (2009).

in durable goods output. However, including the Great Recession, it appears that the relationship between output, sales and inventories partially reverted to the pre-Great Moderation pattern. The covariance of inventories and sales turned positive again, suggesting that improved inventory management was not enough to cushion the massive blow of the Great Recession, and in fact exacerbated it. Focusing just on durable goods again, the change in the covariance between inventories and sales accounts for all of the increase in durable goods output volatility we have seen since 2008.

Even looking just at the recovery period since mid-2009 and excluding the Great Recession, the covariance of sales and inventories is much less negative than it was in the original Great Moderation period, suggesting that inventories are doing less to stabilize output than they once were. Of course, more analysis and more time will be needed to come to a definitive answer on this question.

Table 2. Decomposition of Variance of Goods Output

Component	1960-1983	1984-2007	2008-2013	% of Great Moderation decline	% of post-2008 increase	09:Q2-13:Q4, excl. recession
Goods						
var(output)	13.0	2.3	5.6			1.9
var(sales)	4.8	2.1	2.6	25%	16%	0.5
var(inventories)	7.3	2.4	2.5	46%	2%	2.6
2*cov(sales, inventories)	0.9	-2.2	0.5	29%	82%	-1.2
Durable Goods						
var(output)	9.3	1.5	2.7			0.4
var(sales)	3.2	1.7	1.2	19%	-37%	0.2
var(inventories)	4.3	1.7	1.1	34%	-42%	0.7
2*cov(sales, inventories)	1.8	-1.9	0.3	46%	180%	-0.5

However, I should note that even before the Great Recession, there were serious challenges being posed to the inventory management hypothesis. One of the main challenges drew heavily on data from the automotive sector, showing that one did not need to rely on improved inventory management to explain the reduction in output volatility observed in that industry (Vine and Ramey 2006). Later on, when I return to talk about stabilization policy, I will say a bit more about the volatility of the automotive sector and the President's decision to rescue the auto industry.

What Role Has Financial Innovation Played?

Disaggregating the GDP data, the reduced volatility of consumption is one of the major sources of the Great Moderation—and this reduced volatility has continued to hold up during and after the Great Recession, especially in consumer durables. The continued stability in consumption stands in contrast to other components of GDP like business fixed investment, which became less volatile during the initial Great Moderation but has since at least partially reverted to its earlier volatility.

Reduced consumption volatility originally led Doug Elmendorf, now Director of the Congressional Budget Office (CBO), Karen Dynan, now a senior Treasury official, and Dan Sichel (2006) to posit that financial innovation had made it easier for households to borrow and smooth consumption, thereby contributing to the Great Moderation. This possibility was initially raised by Brad DeLong and Larry Summers (1986), who considered data from 1899 to1982 and found that a smaller share of consumption in the postwar period was accounted for by liquidity-constrained consumers, leading them to argue that, in addition to more robust automatic stabilizers, financial intermediation may have contributed to the moderation in consumption.[8]

The Great Recession, however, showed that financial innovation also makes it possible to create and magnify a shock that can lead to a large downturn in economic activity. So first and foremost, we have to acknowledge that the financial innovation hypothesis can appear to be true in normal times even as the practices it identifies are increasing the chances of greater instability in the future. In a later paper, Dynan (2009) argued that while the decades leading up to the mid-1990s saw a gradual rise in indebtedness that was likely a net positive for households and economic stability, the same cannot be said of the sharper increase in debt that occurred from the mid-1990s until 2007.

In the aftermath of the Great Recession, it is clear that consumers in the aggregate have massively reduced their credit card debt, and cash-out refinancings have fallen substantially. If the original Dynan, Elmendorf and Sichel (2006) hypothesis was correct, then we would expect to have seen aggregate consumption become noticeably more volatile over the last several years, as households have had less opportunity to use credit to smooth consumption. However, this does not appear to be the case. Figure 4 presents the twenty-quarter rolling standard deviation of quarterly real GDP growth that was in Figure 1, along with the same metric for real consumption growth. Puzzlingly, the rise in consumption volatility during and after the Great Recession appears quite muted, both relative to its own historical levels, and to the rise in the volatility of overall GDP growth. But in a period of tight credit conditions, what, then, could explain such relative stability in consumption? This is potentially a very interesting question for future research.

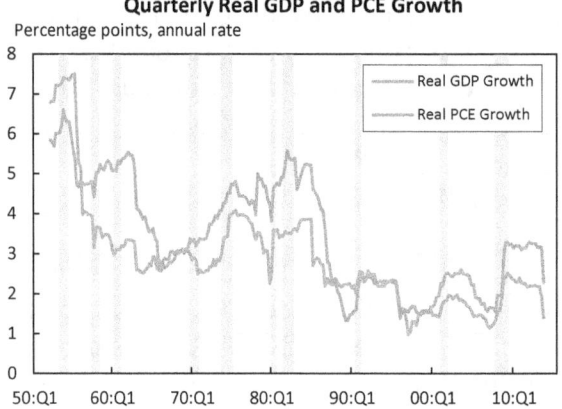

Figure 4. Five-Year Rolling Standard Deviation of Quarterly Real GDP and PCE Growth

Percentage points, annual rate

---

[8] Some have argued that at least part of the reduction in volatility observed in the postwar business cycle is a consequence of improvements in the measurement of key economic indicators since the prewar era. See Romer (1986a, 1986b, 1989, 1991) and Shapiro (1988).

Redefining Moderation: The Importance of Tail Events

Looking at the metrics that were originally used to establish the "Great Moderation" it would seem that, while the economy continues to exhibit substantial month-to-month and year-to-year fluctuations, the volatility of a number of key series have actually returned to—and perhaps even extended—the previous moderation. This suggests that many of the same forces we were discussing prior to 2008 could still be present and stabilizing the economy, with some of the caveats I just discussed.

In this vein, the Great Recession did not outright refute the Great Moderation hypothesis as it was originally proposed. But, the Great Recession certainly does reveal serious limitations of the concept of a Great Moderation. After all, there is no sense in which the recession itself—which witnessed the largest peak-to-trough downturn in GDP on record—was indicative of a more stable economy than in the 1950s or 1960s.

The issue is that the statistics shown in Figure 1 and Table 1 and predominately used in the previous literature are for fluctuations at a quarterly or annual frequency. But these can gloss over lower-frequency events which are the major concern of macroeconomic stabilization, particularly the larger and more persistent tail events that risk reducing us to a lower path of growth and were the focus of Minsky's work. And the Great Recession was, of course, the largest and longest downturn we have had in eighty years.

One way of conveying this distinction is to update two graphs from Bob Hall's (2003) comment on the Stock and Watson paper. Figure 5a shows the volatility of one year changes in GDP, as measured by the absolute difference between the one-year real GDP growth and its long-term average. Like the results above, it spiked up during the Great Recession but has since come back down and exhibits the very muted pattern characteristic of the last several recoveries, as growth after the downturn has recently remained close to the long-term average. But looking at the absolute deviation of ten-year GDP growth from its long-term average, Figure 5b shows a very different picture—depicting a tremendous and sustained increase in volatility exceeding the most volatile point just before the Great Moderation. It can be somewhat counterintuitive to think of "volatility" in a ten-year change, but that is precisely what we are seeing right now, even in the recovery.

Figure 5a. Absolute Deviation of One-Year GDP Growth From Its Full-Sample Average

Figure 5b. Absolute Deviation of Ten-Year GDP Growth From Its Full-Sample Average

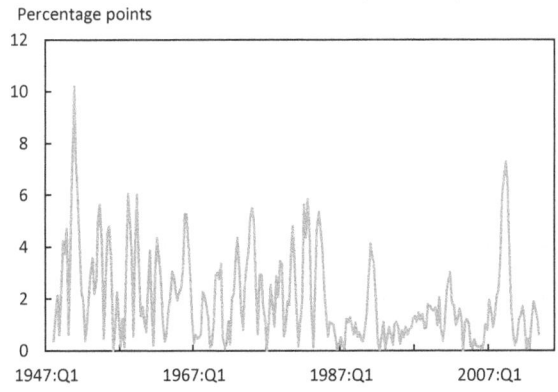

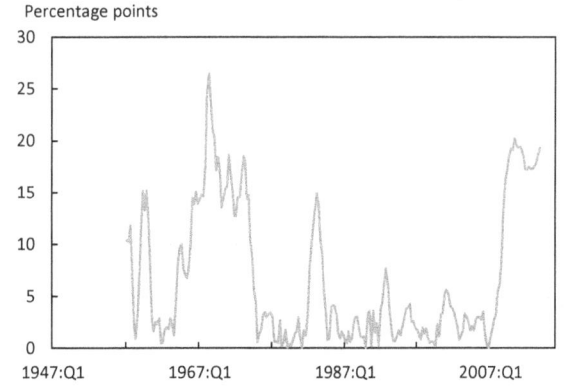

It is much harder to make statistical inferences about rare events, especially when the structure of the economy and policy itself is changing—and changing in part because of policy responses to these rare events like the Dodd-Frank Wall Street Reform Act, which I will discuss later. That said, based on recent experience it would be foolish to be complacent and fully assume that in the deeper, lower frequency sense there ever was a genuine "Great Moderation," let alone that it has returned and renders further policy steps unnecessary. But before discussing the unfinished policy agenda for macroeconomic stabilization, let me briefly describe why macroeconomic stability is so important.

Why Moderation Matters

The proposition that large fluctuations in output are problematic and worth addressing should not be controversial. In some academic circles, however, a number of theories have been advanced that question this premise. These theories have real-world analogues, playing into arguments against macroeconomic stabilization policies. For this reason it is worth briefly discussing some of the main arguments.

The first objection to stabilization policy is that output fluctuations are optimal or nearly irrelevant. The stronger version of this view is real business cycle theory, which posits that fluctuations are optimal responses to productivity and taste shocks,[9] an idea that flies in the face of the patently sub-optimal results that are recessions. Some of the more extreme policy implications of this view are generally not taken as seriously anymore, even in freshwater circles, which often accept that a variety of market or government imperfections allow for the possibility of sub-optimal equilibria.

The weaker version of this view is associated with Robert Lucas (1987, 2003), who undertook a calibration exercise showing that assuming perfect insurance and a particular utility function, then a person would only be willing to give up less than 0.1 percent of his or her lifetime consumption to avoid volatility in consumption generated by aggregate economic fluctuations. A number of responses have been made to this claim, including technical objections to Lucas's assumption about the degree of risk aversion people exhibit, as well as a recalibration of the same exercise that recognizes the possibility of rare disasters.[10]

But one of the most fundamental issues with Lucas's calculation is that it assumes a representative agent (or equivalently perfect insurance), so that in his model a downturn means that everyone is consuming 5 percent less—not that 5 percent of the people lose their jobs, their earnings power, and thus see a much larger hit to their consumption. As a number of researchers have pointed out, people would pay a lot more to avoid this risk.[11] Moreover, this risk is not spread identically across the economy because downturns disproportionately hurt the most vulnerable groups. Figure 6 shows the well-known pattern of black and Hispanic unemployment

---

[9] See, for example, Kydland and Prescott (1977)
[10] See, for example, Alvarez and Jermann (2004) and Barro (2009)
[11] See Barlevy (2005) for an overview.

rates rising much higher than white unemployment rates in recessions and falling back slowly in recoveries, albeit with a persistent gap.

Figure 6. Gap Between Black-White and Hispanic-White Unemployment Rates

Percentage points

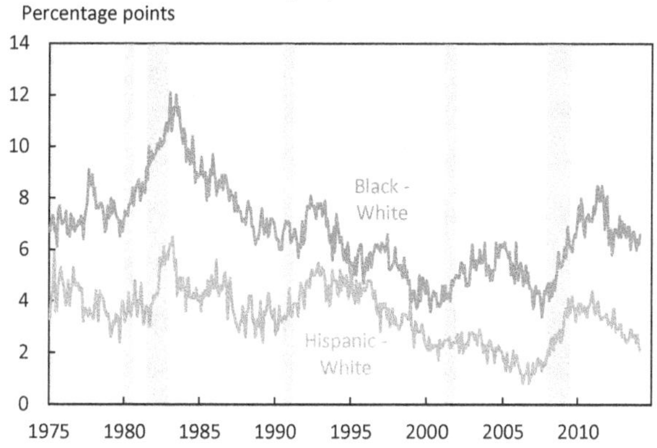

The second objection to stabilization policy is that output fluctuations are actually supportive of future growth—as Joseph Schumpeter (1934) famously noted "[recessions] are but temporary. They are the means to reconstruct each time the economic system on a more efficient plan." In other words, the relative return of productive activities to productivity-enhancing activities falls in a recession, increasing the return to the latter and thus fostering more innovation. Theory and evidence, however, suggest the opposite is true. As Garey Ramey and Valerie Ramey (1991) argued in an early reply to Lucas, higher volatility can be harmful for growth because increased uncertainty reduces investment, especially when firms must commit in advance to a certain scale of production. On a similar note, Barlevy (2007) shows that even though it might be rational to devote more resources to research and development (R&D) during a downturn when sales are lower, the empirical fact is that R&D activity is pro-cyclical, which compounds the cost of negative macroeconomic shocks. Moreover, the relationship between growth and volatility is much more nuanced than the original Schumpeterian formulation allows for. Research by Philippe Aghion and others, for example, has linked long-run growth with credit constraints, cyclical fiscal policy, and exchange rates, all of which are used to attempt to account for the observed inconsistency between Schumpeter's claim and the observed behavior of countries and industries.[12]

DeLong and Summers (1988) also pointed out that stabilization policy is not symmetric; rather, it means that the economy spends less time operating well below potential and thus increases average output. This observation is also another flaw in Lucas's calculation of the welfare cost of business cycle fluctuations, which assumed that fluctuations had no impact on the average level of output.

Finally, a third objection to stabilization policy is that even if fluctuations are undesirable for distributional reasons and harmful (or neutral) for growth, there is still nothing we can do about them. This view goes back at least to President Herbert Hoover, was formalized by Milton Friedman (1953), and has unfortunately been the theory most often advanced against efforts to

---

[12] See, for example, Aghion et al. (2006), Aghion, Hemous and Kharroubi (2009), and Aghion et al. (2010)

combat the Great Recession.[13] While this general set of ideas was a useful caution against attempts to fine-tune the economy in more normal times, it is a potentially dangerous perspective when the economy is clearly operating below potential and, despite progress, will be operating below potential for a sustained period of time.

In fact, I believe policymakers have and can continue to do something about economic fluctuations. The next section discusses some of the progress and unfinished business in that area.

The Unfinished Agenda for Economic Stability

Improvements in monetary and fiscal policy have likely contributed to the patterns in the high-frequency data originally identified as the Great Moderation, although one could debate the share of the credit they deserve. I believe policy steps have also played a critical role at lower frequencies as well, with the best example being the Great Recession itself, which in many ways started off looking like it could be as bad or worse than the Great Depression. To appreciate this point, consider that the plunge in stock prices in late 2008 proved similar to what occurred in late 1929, but was compounded by sharper home price declines, ultimately leading to a drop in overall household wealth that was substantially greater than the loss in wealth at the outset of the Great Depression (Romer 2009). The crisis had global reverberations, and world trade volumes fell even more sharply from mid-2008 to mid-2009 than they did in the early stages of the Great Depression (Almunia, et al. 2010). Moreover, Alan Greenspan (2013) has argued that short-term credit markets froze more severely in 2008 than in 1929, and to find a comparable episode in this regard one has to go back to the panic of 1907. However, in large part because of an aggressive policy response, the unemployment rate increased 5 percentage points, compared to a more than 20 percentage point increase in the Great Depression from 1929 to 1934. And real GDP per working age population returned to its pre-recession peak more quickly in the United States than in other countries that also experienced systemic crises in 2007-08.

And it was not just fiscal and monetary policies that made a difference: the rescue of the automobile industry is an important part of the story in both preventing a second Great Depression and in increasing overall economic stability in the recovery. Before the recession, Vine and Ramey (2006) pointed out that since the 1960s, motor vehicle production accounted for almost 25 percent of the variance of aggregate GDP growth even though motor vehicle production represented less than 5 percent of GDP on average. One implication of this striking fact is that a more stable auto sector can go a long way towards stabilizing the overall economy, and that is exactly what we have seen in the recovery. Looking since mid-2009, the variance of real GDP growth *increases* by nearly a quarter if you exclude the motor vehicle sector—that is to say the auto sector has actually reduced economic volatility.

Nevertheless, significant hardship has been caused by the Great Recession and despite steady progress it continues to linger today. Much of the response to the Great Recession was necessarily *ad hoc* and improvised with policymakers being forced to develop unprecedented new tools and approaches to address an unprecedented situation. As the economy continues to

---

[13] See Taylor (2009).

heal, now is the time to continue working on what can be done to put us in a better position to prevent or respond to future downturns. We have made progress in fostering macroeconomic stability, but there is a great deal of unfinished business.

Discussions about improving macroeconomic stability have often centered on monetary policy, both on questions of alternative rules and the way it is implemented in practice. I will not have anything to say about monetary policy, not because it is unimportant but because it is a topic that I am institutionally and appropriately precluded from commenting on. Moreover, in focusing nearly exclusively on monetary policy, some of the discussions of macroeconomic stabilization have underemphasized a number of other areas that are also important. I will focus on four of these areas. I should note that for some of the areas I will discuss, macroeconomic stability is not the primary purpose—for instance, we also care about seeing the economy grow faster, and about ensuring that growth is broadly shared. Nevertheless, my hope is that considering some of the policies through the lens of macroeconomic stability can shed light on some of their underappreciated benefits and in some cases affect how we think about designing the policies themselves.

Improving Fiscal Stabilizers—From the Affordable Care Act to Broader Fiscal Policies

Many economists have a long-standing skepticism of discretionary countercyclical fiscal policy, citing recognition lags, implementation lags, impact lags, and political constraints (e.g., Taylor 2000). A more widely but still not universally accepted exception is when monetary policy is constrained at the zero lower bound and the output gap is large and persistent. In this context, the usual lags are not an objection to discretionary fiscal policy and the multiplier may be larger (e.g., DeLong and Summers 2012). Moreover, by preventing permanent damage to the economy's growth path and investing in things like infrastructure that enhance long-run growth, discretionary fiscal policy can in certain macroeconomic environments largely pay for itself. In the current cycle, the evidence suggests that discretionary fiscal policy played a critical role in helping stabilize the economy more quickly than normal following a systemic financial crisis (Council of Economic Advisers 2014). But as shown in Figure 7, automatic stabilizers also played a quantitatively important role, representing about half of the fiscal expansion from 2009 through 2012.

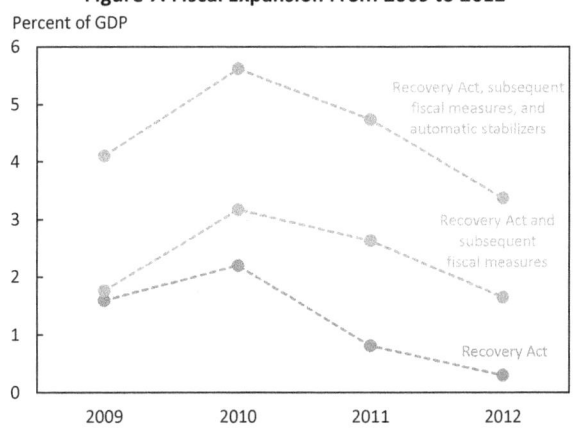

Figure 7. Fiscal Expansion From 2009 to 2012

The Administration has meaningfully strengthened the automatic stabilizers in the last several years. The Affordable Care Act (ACA) is not normally thought of as a countercyclical macroeconomic policy, but it is. The combination of progressive tax credits and the Medicaid expansion will significantly help households smooth consumption and will expand aggregate demand when it would otherwise be impaired. Although macroeconomic stabilization was not the goal of the ACA, its benefits in that regard are not an accident either. In general, policies that strengthen social insurance, helping people when their incomes are lower, will also have a broader macroeconomic benefit in the form of increased stability. In that vein, the additional progressivity in the tax code we have implemented—including expanded refundable tax credits for lower-income households and higher tax rates for high-income households—also contribute to automatic stabilization.

Going forward it is worth exploring whether there are further steps that would expand automatic stabilizers, and strengthen the countercyclical features of other key programs, including means-tested programs.

Additionally, as we think about the significant challenge of elevated long-term unemployment today, these types of steps to enhance the automatic stabilizers would help prevent more individuals from experiencing extended spells of unemployment, and to the degree we cannot prevent it, we should provide them with support as they continue to look for jobs. That particular priority is especially important today, as the House of Representatives now has the opportunity act on the Senate-passed bill that would reinstate extended unemployment insurance benefits for the more than 2 million people who have seen their benefits expire since the beginning of the year as they continue to look for jobs.

Reducing Inequality as a Macroeconomic Stability Measure

One of the major frontiers for researchers is to develop a better understanding of the link between macroeconomic performance and inequality. Economists at the IMF have identified a link in cross-country data between lower inequality and longer periods of growth (Berg and Ostry 2011), generalizing a story that Raghuram Rajan (2010) told in his book *Fault Lines*. Other IMF work has shown that steps taken to reduce inequality are in and of themselves generally benign with respect to growth, and in fact are pro-growth when their inequality-reducing effects are taken into account (Ostry, Berg, and Tsangarides 2014). But we still have a lot more to learn in this area.

Looking at the United States over the last several years, the challenge right now is not to stabilize consumption—it has actually been quite stable since the recession—but to strengthen it. And one way to do that is to boost incomes for lower-income households, which have a higher marginal propensity to consume on average. The Administration has proposed a range of measures, from short-run steps like raising the minimum wage, to longer-run proposals like expanding access to preschool, that ultimately seek to grow wages and expand economic opportunity for low-income households. But even as the current focus remains on strengthening rather than stabilizing consumption, we should not lose sight of the fact that these sorts of actions can also have a stabilizing effect. Rising incomes put households in a better position to build financial assets that they can use to smooth consumption in the face of unexpected disruptions to their income, helping to prevent borrowing bubbles, while at the same time creating a broader, more stable foundation for aggregate consumer spending growth.

Drawing on another IMF study (Kumhof, Ranciere and Winant 2013), Figure 8 presents the aggregate household debt-to-GDP ratio for the U.S. economy, and the share of income going to the top 5 percent of earners.[14] While I concede that this picture vastly oversimplifies an incredibly complex web of economic issues, it is striking that the run-ups to two high points in income inequality were matched by run-ups in household debt. While this does not establish anything causal, it does highlight the importance of continuing to think about the link between inequality and macroeconomic stabilization.

Figure 8. Top 5 Percent Income Share and Aggregate Debt-to-GDP Ratio

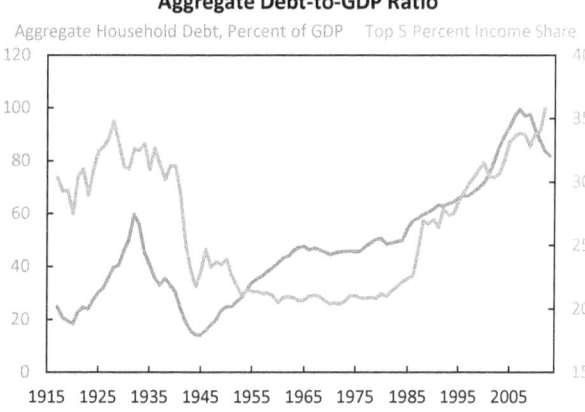

Improving Financial Stability—and the Unfinished Business of Housing Finance Reform

The Great Recession was caused by a financial crisis that had many dimensions, including overborrowing by households, risky securities, undercapitalized banks, and runs on key markets. The Dodd-Frank Wall Street Reform and Consumer Protection Act and complementary reforms are designed to provide multiple firewalls against future financial crises, including reducing chances to make systemic errors through better consumer protections, limits on certain risky activities, and systemic oversight; reducing the risk that bad decisions would lead to the failure of a bank through higher capital standards; reducing the risk that a bank failure would be a systemic event through better resolution mechanisms; and ultimately ensuring that no matter what happens taxpayers will not be on the hook for bailouts.

The most important piece of unfinished business in the financial arena is housing finance reform. There is no doubt that the housing system contributed to the financial crisis. And while placing Fannie Mae and Freddie Mac in conservatorship and infusing them with liquidity in the midst of the Great Recession has helped to foster a housing recovery, further progress will best be served by moving forward with a system that puts private capital at risk, protects

---

[14] Data on household liabilities prior to 1952 are taken from Saez and Kopczuk (2004). Top 5 percent income share from the 2013 update to Piketty and Saez (2003). GDP data prior to 1929 are taken from the *Historical Statistics of the United States*.

15

homeowners, creates a vibrant competitive marketplace, and includes transparent support for broader homeownership.

In addition to all of these goals, one critical and sometimes underappreciated goal of a reformed system is that it should enhance macroeconomic stability. The residential sector has historically been one of the most cyclically volatile, and, as was acutely felt in the Great Recession, this volatility can take a severe toll on all Americans homeowners but especially those middle-income families that have a disproportionate share of wealth in their homes. Housing finance reform can thus play a critical role by providing both a structure that makes housing finance, and in turn the housing sector, more cyclically resilient, and also providing a mechanism that helps lean against the wind of the worst downturns in housing.

The motivation behind cyclical resilience is straightforward: even if the economy is in a downturn, and even if there are disruptions to financial markets, the housing finance system should still continue providing reasonably-priced mortgages to creditworthy borrowers. Instead, even to this day, roughly five years after the Great Recession, lending standards remain tight and many creditworthy borrowers are still unable to get a mortgage. The natural cyclical volatility of housing should not continue abetted by financial market failures that stifle lending in the mortgage market.

Encouraging cyclical resilience means ensuring that the structural pipelines through which credit flows from the secondary market to mortgage originators are exposed to limited credit risk. It also means setting up an institutional structure in which the Federal government can expand quickly in the event of a financial market disruption or economic downturn from its ideally remote position to one that temporarily ensures funds keep flowing to qualified borrowers. Finally, it entails an institutional structure that greatly minimizes the chances of government bailouts, so that private participants do not have an incentive to take excessive risks. The perceived implicit guarantee and legal advantages conferred on government-sponsored enterprises before the recession lowered their cost of funding relative to their competitors and allowed them to capture large shares of the market to the point where they became too big to fail. It is critical that we do not allow history to repeat itself at the expense of the taxpayer. It is also critical that we do not eliminate any fee-financed government backstop entirely, both because of what this would do the functioning of housing markets but also because it would not be a credible commitment and would almost inevitably result in an *ad hoc*, taxpayer-financed bailout the next time the system ran into serious problems.

Putting all these pieces together is a complex undertaking. However, the current period provides an opportunity in which major steps can be taken on the long path of reform. The Senate Banking Committee is making promising bipartisan progress and the Administration looks forward to continuing to work with Congress to forge a new private housing finance system that better serves current and future generations of Americans.

Macroeconomic stability does not just depend on policy steps in the United States. We know full well that international crises can have spillover effects that have a major impact on the U.S. economy and the interests of our companies abroad. Our first line of defense against these crises is the IMF, which has been central to the stability of the international financial system since World War II. In 2010, G-20 leaders and IMF members agreed to a landmark set of reforms to modernize and strengthen the IMF. These reforms ensure the IMF has the resources the Fund needs to safeguard the global economy and give a greater voice to dynamic emerging economies that want to play a greater role in the international financial system. That is very much in the interests of the United States. These reforms are critical to ensure our leadership in the IMF, which is central to the promotion of our national security and economic interests around the world. Ratification in the U.S. Congress is the final step before these reforms can go into effect, and Congress's failure to act jeopardizes our influence in the IMF and undermines our international leadership.

Beyond the IMF's role in managing immediate crises, it is also worth noting that developing economies around the world can benefit from improved macroeconomic stabilization policies, including the types of steps I have been talking about in the context of the United States. More broadly, steps that foster income growth and development tend to increase macroeconomic stability by creating a more diversified economy and increasing the ability of households to insure against shocks.

Without making any claim to have determined the direction of causality, Figure 9 shows the relationship between countries' economic volatility and level of income, plotting the log of real per capita GDP in 2013 in purchasing power parity terms against the standard deviation of yearly real per capita GDP growth from 1981-2013.[15] What is particularly striking is the overall negative relationship and the cluster of countries in the upper left with high income and low volatility, including the United States, Canada, Japan, Australia, and much of Western Europe.

---

[15] The chart includes 131 countries for which the IMF has complete yearly data going back to 1980. It excludes four outliers with standard deviation of yearly GDP growth in excess of 10 (Kuwait, Lebanon, Libya, and Sudan). A similar figure appears in Koren and Tenreyro (2007).

Figure 9. Cross Country Comparison of Income and Volatility

Log of ppp-adjusted per capita GDP, 2013

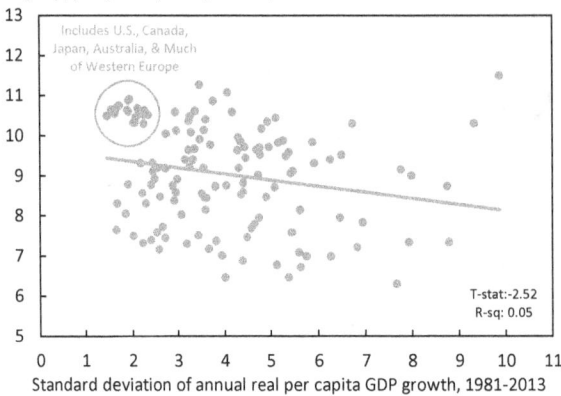

Standard deviation of annual real per capita GDP growth, 1981-2013

Conclusion

As turbulent as the economy can seem from day-to-day or from month-to-month, it is important to put these higher frequency fluctuations in perspective. A combination of true volatility associated with everything from animal spirits to weather to high-frequency feedback cycles will always impact the economy. But, if anything, these shocks are smaller today and we are better able to control them. In part, this represents a substantial public policy accomplishment.

But the Great Recession, at the very least, put the declaration of victory on the Great Moderation in substantial perspective. There is much more to macroeconomic stabilization than smoothing quarterly or annual fluctuations—the ultimate goal is to address the largest and most persistent fluctuations. In the case of the Great Recession, policy partly failed to do that, although the fact that we avoided a second Great Depression is a testament to improvements in macroeconomic and financial policy.

Ultimately, our most fundamental concern is with strengthening growth—both in the short run as the economy returns to its potential and over the longer run as we aim to expand that potential—while ensuring that everyone shares in that growth. But macroeconomic stabilization, especially for the larger, lower frequency tail events, is both an important end in itself as well as generally a complement to these other goals. There is no doubt that going through another Great Recession would not only risk substantial damage to the economy, but would have a substantial human toll. As we continue to dig out of the Great Recession, we can also continue to look forward to what we can do to prevent, mitigate or ameliorate the potential for a next one at some future date.

Bibliography

Aghion, P., Angeletos, G. M., Banerjee, A., & Manova, K. (2010). Volatility and growth: Credit constraints and the composition of investment. *Journal of Monetary Economics, 57*(3), 246-265.

Aghion, P., Bacchetta, P., Ranciere, R., & Rogoff, K. (2009). Exchange rate volatility and productivity growth: the role of financial development. *Journal of Monetary Economics, 56*(4), 494-513.

Aghion, P., Hemous, D., & Kharroubi, E. (2009). *Credit constraints, cyclical fiscal policy and industry growth* (No. w15119). National Bureau of Economic Research.

Ahmed, S., Levin, A., & Wilson, B. A. (2004). Recent US macroeconomic stability: good policies, good practices, or good luck? *Review of Economics and Statistics, 86*(3), 824-832.

Almunia, M., Benetrix, A., Eichengreen, B., O'Rourke, K. H., & Rua, G. (2010). From great depression to great credit crisis: similarities, differences and lessons. *Economic Policy, 25*(62), 219-265.

Barlevy, G. (2007). On the cyclicality of research and development. *The American Economic Review*, 1131-1164.

Bernanke, B. S. (2004). The great moderation: Remarks by Governor Ben S. Bernanke at the meetings of the Eastern Economic Association, Washington, DC February 20, 2004. *Eastern Economic Association, Washington, DC, 20.*

Blanchard, O., & Simon, J. (2001). The long and large decline in US output volatility. *Brookings Papers on Economic Activity, 2001*(1), 135-174.

Council of Economic Advisers (2014). *The Economic Report of the President.*

Davis, S. J., & Kahn, J. A. (2008). *Interpreting the great moderation: Changes in the volatility of economic activity at the macro and micro levels* (No. w14048). National Bureau of Economic Research.

DeLong, J. B., & Summers, L. H. (1986). The changing cyclical variability of economic activity in the United States. In *The American Business Cycle: Continuity and Change* (pp. 679-734). University of Chicago Press.

DeLong, J. B., Summers, L. H. (1988). How does macroeconomic policy affect output? *Brookings Papers on Economic Activity*, 433-494.

DeLong, J. B., Summers, L. H. (2012). Fiscal Policy in a Depressed Economy [with Comments and Discussion]. *Brookings Papers on Economic Activity*, 233-297.

Dynan, K. E. (2009). Changing household financial opportunities and economic security. *The Journal of Economic Perspectives*, 49-68.

Dynan, K. E., Elmendorf, D. W., & Sichel, D. E. (2006). Can financial innovation help to explain the reduced volatility of economic activity? *Journal of Monetary Economics*, *53*(1), 123-150.

Friedman, M. (1953). "The Effects of Full Employment Policy on Economic Stability: A Formal Analysis." *Essays in Positive Economics*, Chicago: Univ. of Chicago Press, 117-132.

Gadea, M. D., Gómez-Loscos, A., & Pérez-Quirós, G. (2013). Has the Great Recession ousted the Great Moderation?

Greenspan, A. (2013). *The Map and the Territory: Risk, Human Nature, and the Future of Forecasting*. Penguin.

Kahn, J. A., McConnell, M. M., & Perez-Quiros, G. (2002). On the Causes of the Increased Stability of the US Economy. *Federal Reserve Bank of New York Economic Policy Review*, *8*(1), 183-202.

Kim, C. J., & Nelson, C. R. (1999). Has the US economy become more stable? A Bayesian approach based on a Markov-switching model of the business cycle. *Review of Economics and Statistics*, *81*(4), 608-616.

Koren, M. & Tenreyro, S. (2007). "Volatility and Development." *The Quarterly Journal of Economics* 122 (1), 243-287.

Kumhof, M., Ranciere, R., & Winant, P. (2013). "Inequality, Leverage and Crises: The Case of Endogenous Default." (No. 13/249). International Monetary Fund.

Lucas, R. E. (1987). *Models of business cycles* (Vol. 26). Oxford: Basil Blackwell.

Lucas, R. E. (2003). Macroeconomic priorities. *American Economic Review*, *93* (1), 1-14.

McCarthy, J., & Zakrajšek, E. (2007). Inventory dynamics and business cycles: what has changed? *Journal of Money, Credit and Banking*, *39*(2-3), 591-613.

McConnell, M. M., & Perez-Quiros, G. (2000). Output fluctuations in the United States: What has changed since the early 1980's? *American Economic Review*, 1464-1476.

Ostry, J. D., & Berg, A. (2011). *Inequality and unsustainable growth: two sides of the same coin?* (No. 11/08). International Monetary Fund.

Ostry, M. J. D., Berg, M. A., & Tsangarides, M. C. G. (2014). *Redistribution, Inequality, and Growth*. International Monetary Fund.

Piketty, T. & Saez, E. (2003). "Income Inequality in the United States 1913–1998." *Quarterly Journal of Economics* 118, no. 1: 1–39.

Piketty, T. & Saez, E. (2013). Data update to "Income Inequality in the United States 1913–1998."

Rajan, R.G. (2010). *Fault Lines: How Hidden Fractures Still Threaten the World Economy*. Princeton University Press.

Ramey, G., & Ramey, V. A. (1991). *Technology commitment and the cost of economic fluctuations* (No. w3755). National Bureau of Economic Research.

Ramey, V. A., & Vine, D. J. (2006). Declining volatility in the US automobile industry. *The American Economic Review*, 1876-1889.

Romer, C. (2009). Lessons from the Great Depression for economic recovery in 2009.

Romer, C. (1986a). Spurious Volatility in Historical Unemployment Data. *Journal of Political Economy*, 97(1), 1-37.

Romer, C. (1986b). Is the Stabilization of the Postwar Economy a Figment of the Data? *American Economic Review*, 76(3), 314-34.

Romer, C. (1989). The Prewar Business Cycle Reconsidered: New Estimates of Gross National Product, 1869-1908. *Journal of Political Economy*, 97(1), 1-37.

Romer, C. (1991). The Cyclical Behavior of Individual Production Series, 1889-1984. *The Quarterly Journal of Economics*, 106(1), 1-31.

Saez, E. & Kopczuk, W. (2004). "Top Wealth Shares in the United States, 1916-2000: Evidence from Estate Tax Returns." *National Tax Journal* 57 (2), 445-487.

Schumpeter, J. A. (1934). Depressions. *Douglass V. Brown, et al., The Economics of the Recovery Program. New York: Whittlesey House, McGraw-Hill*, 3-21.

Shapiro, Matthew D. (1988). The Stabilization of the U.S. Economy: Evidence from the Stock Market. *American Economic Review*, 78(5), 1067-1079.

Singh, A., & Morley, J. (2009). Inventory Mistakes and the Great Moderation.

Stock, J. H., & Watson, M. W. (2003). Has the business cycle changed and why? In *NBER Macroeconomics Annual 2002, Volume 17* (pp. 159-230). MIT press.

Taylor, J. B. (2000). Reassessing discretionary fiscal policy. *The Journal of Economic Perspectives*, 21-36.